Learn SignWriting on the web!

Download books & view videos: www.SignWriting.org/lessons

What Is SignWriting?

**With SignWriting,
you can....**

READ
**Sign
Language**

WRITE
**Sign
Language**

PRESERVE
**Sign Poetry
and Theater**

Write SignWriting on the web!

Write signs and Sign Language documents: www.SignPuddle.org

 LEARN Sign Language

 **TRANSCRIBE Sign Language**

 SHARE Sign Language

 MEET Signers Who Write Sign Language Too!

Join the SignWriting Email List!

Go to this web page to join: www.SignWriting.org/forums/swlist

Receptive Viewpoint

When someone is facing you, signing to you, you view the signs as an observer.
The signer's right side is your left side. This is called the **Receptive Viewpoint.**

Expressive Viewpoint

When you are signing to someone else, you see signs from your own point of view.
This is called the **Expressive Viewpoint**.

The Expressive Viewpoint

Read and write signs as if you are looking at your own hands, from your own perspective.

Palm of Hand

When you see the palm of your hand, while you are signing, the symbol for the hand will be white, or hollow.

The palm of the hand is always written with a white, hollow symbol.

Side of Hand

When you see the side of your hand while you are signing, the symbol for the hand will be half black and half white.

The white part of the symbol shows where the palm of the hand faces. The dark part represents the back of the hand.

Back of Hand

When you see the back of your hand while you are signing, the symbol will be black, or filled-in.

The back of the hand is always written with a black, filled-in symbol.

Left Side of Head

The head is written with a circle, viewed from the back. When the left hand is near the left side of the head, the symbol for the hand is placed to the left:

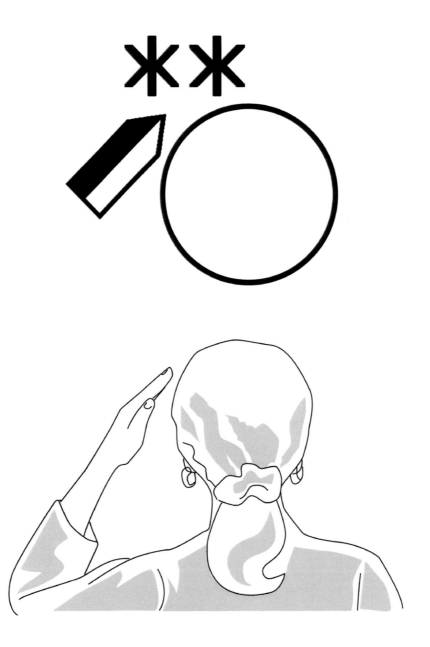

know
(hand on the left side)

Note: An asterisk means **touch**.
Two asterisks mean **touching two times**.

Right Side of Head

The head is written with a circle, viewed from the back. When the right hand is near the right side of the head, the symbol for the hand is placed to the right:

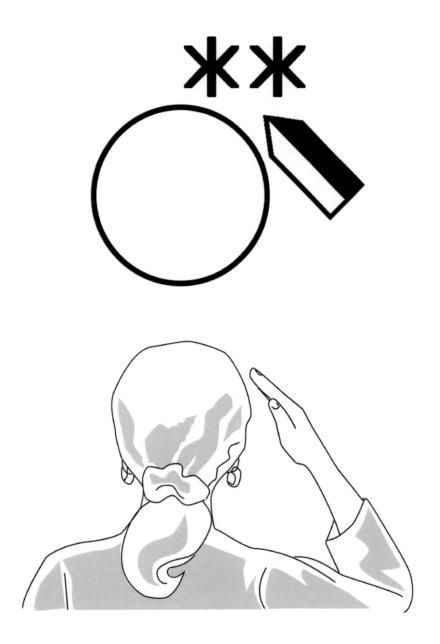

know
(hand on the right side)

Note: An asterisk means **touch**.
Two asterisks mean **touching two times**.

Left Side of Face

Pretend you can see through the back of the head.
You are reading and writing how your face **"feels"** when you sign:

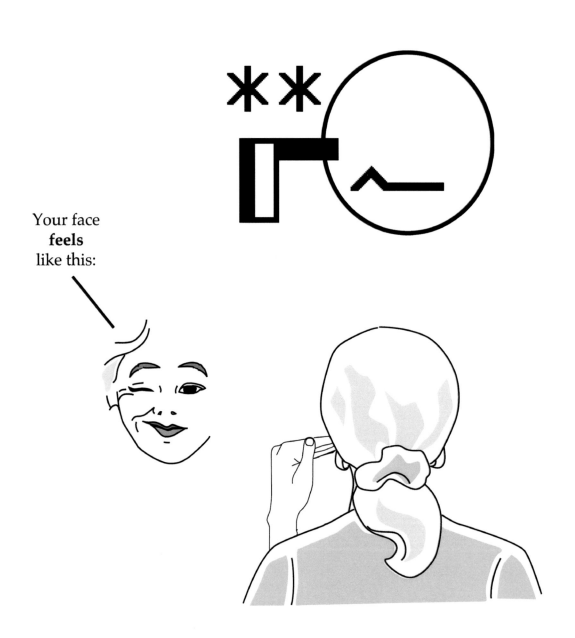

Your face
feels
like this:

know
(mouth pushed up on left side)

Right Side of Face

Pretend you can see through the back of the head.
You are reading and writing how your face **"feels"** when you sign:

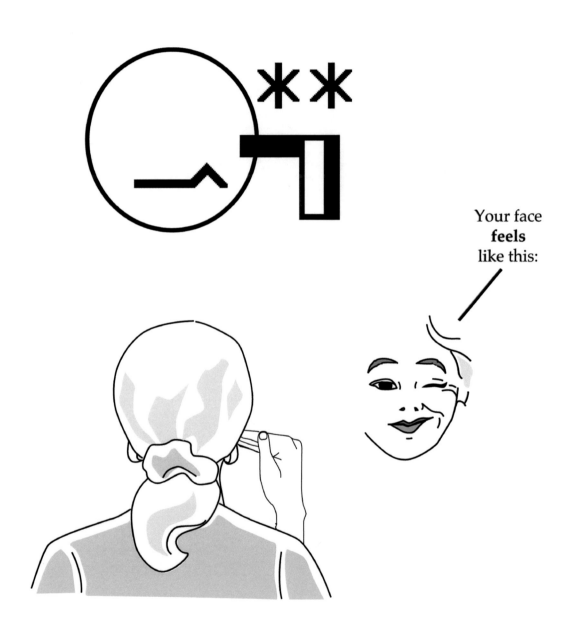

Your face
feels
like this:

know
(mouth pushed up on right side)

3 Basic Handshapes

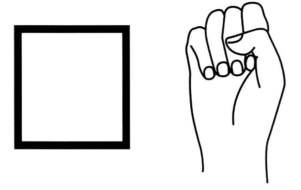

Closed Fist

When the fingertips touch the palm of the hand, it is called a **Closed Fist**.

A **Closed Fist** is written with a square.

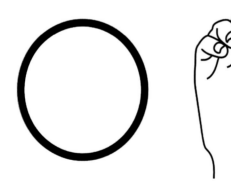

Open Fist

When the fingertips touch each other, it is called an **Open Fist**.

An **Open Fist** is written with a circle.

3 Basic Handshapes

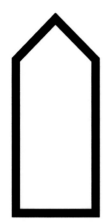

Flat Hand

When the fingers stretch straight up, and touch each other, it is called a **Flat Hand**.

A **Flat Hand** is written with a rectangle, with a tip for the fingertips.

Closed Fist

Both the letter S and the number 1 in ASL are written with a square for the Closed Fist, since the fingertips touch the palm:

Open Fist

Both the letter O and the letter D in ASL are written with a circle for the Open Fist, since the fingertips touch each other:

Palm Facing

Front View

The hand is parallel with the front wall.

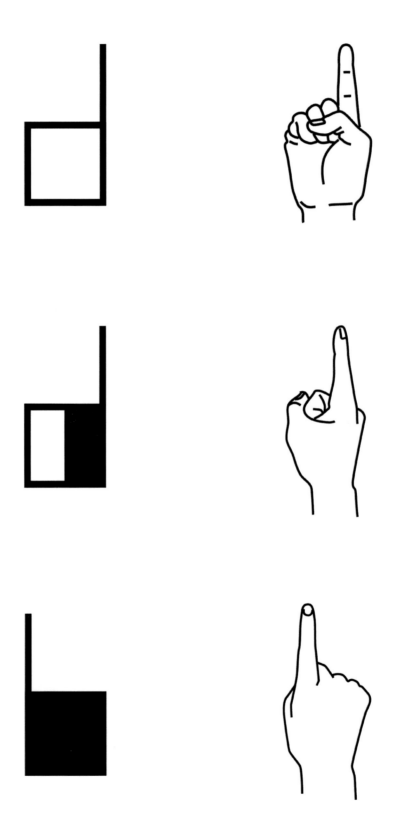

Palm Facing
Top View
The hand is parallel with the floor.

space at
knuckle joint
means hand
is parallel
to the floor

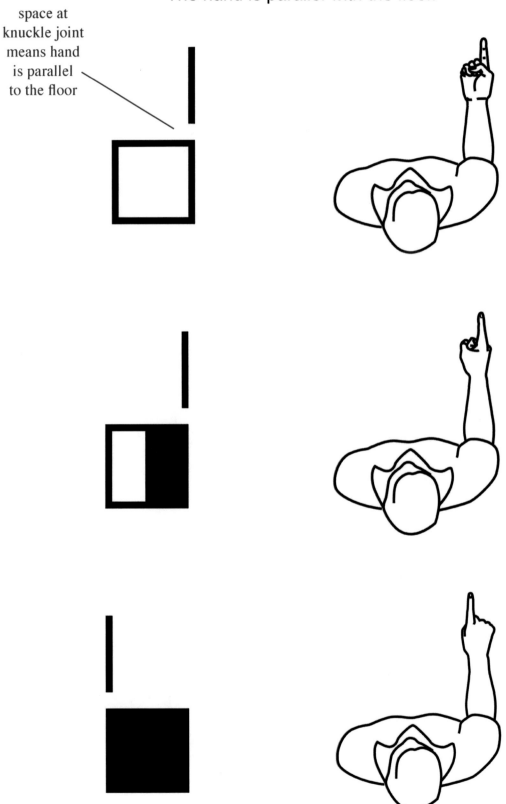

Palm Facing
Front View
The hand is parallel with the front wall.

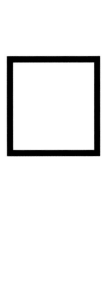 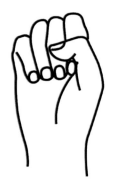

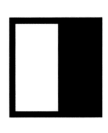 

Palm Facing

Top View
The hand is parallel with the floor.

space at knuckle joint means hand is parallel to the floor

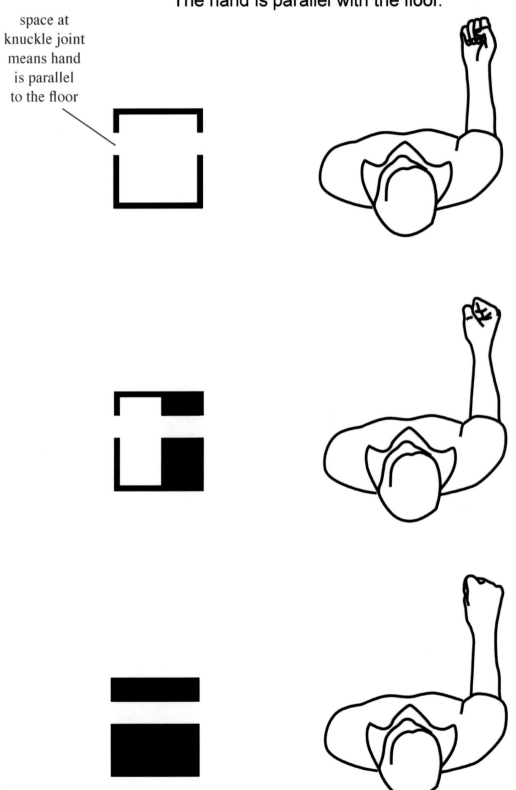

Palm Facing

Front View

The hand is parallel with the front wall.

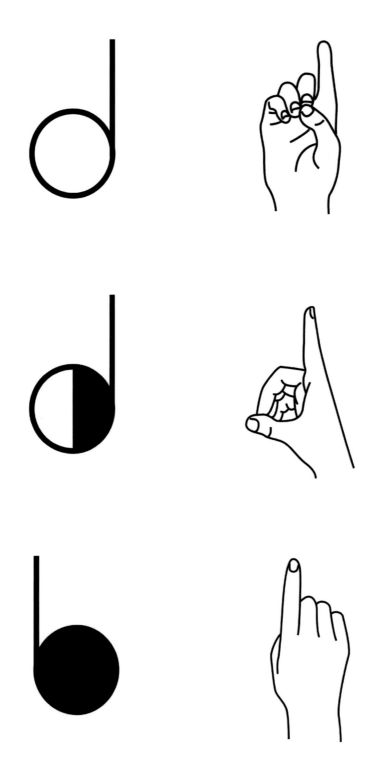

Palm Facing

Top View
The hand is parallel with the floor.

space at
knuckle joint
means hand
is parallel
to the floor

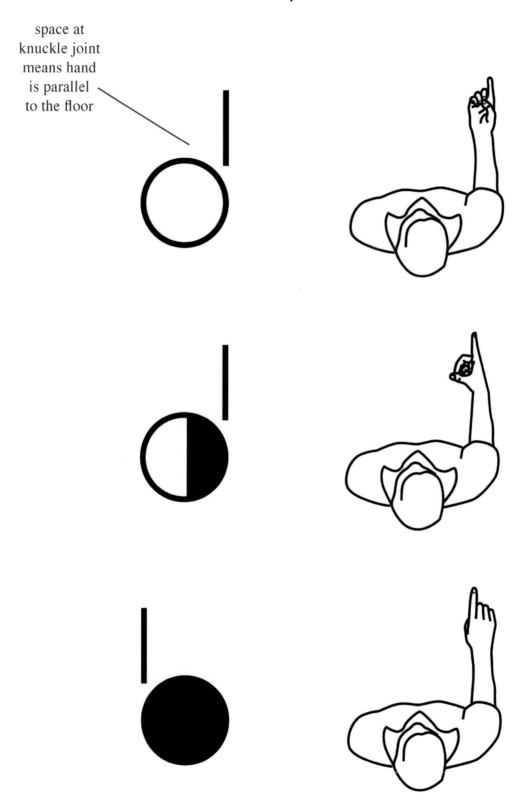

Palm Facing

Front View

The hand is parallel with the front wall.

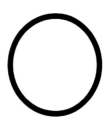 

Palm Facing
Top View
The hand is parallel with the floor.

space at
knuckle joint
means hand
is parallel
to the floor

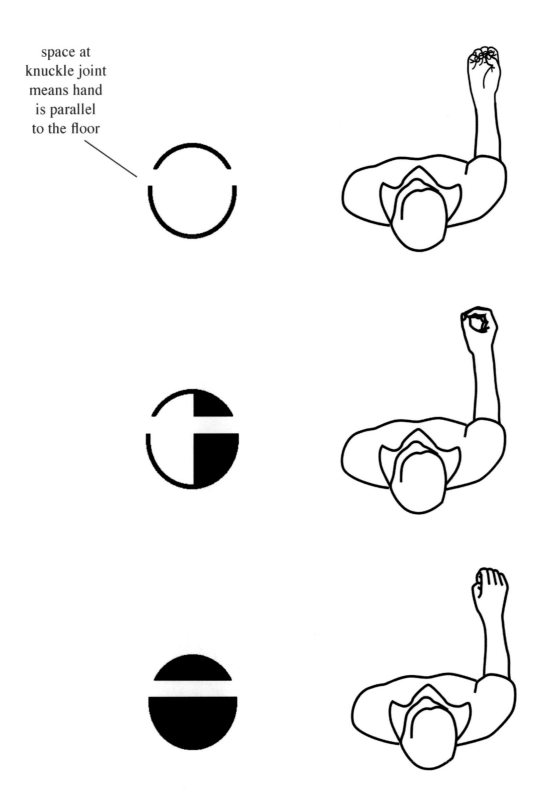

Palm Facing

Front View

The hand is parallel with the front wall.

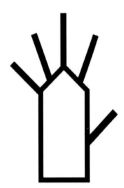 

 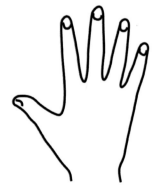

Palm Facing
Top View
The hand is parallel with the floor.

space at
knuckle joint
means hand
is parallel
to the floor

Palm Facing
Front View
The hand is parallel with the front wall.

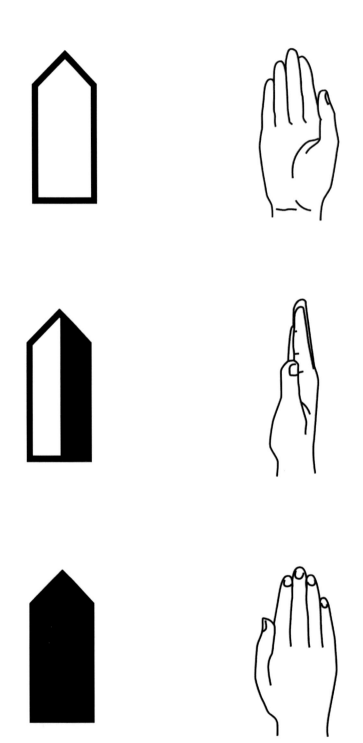

Palm Facing

Top View

The hand is parallel with the floor.

space at
knuckle joint
means hand
is parallel
to the floor

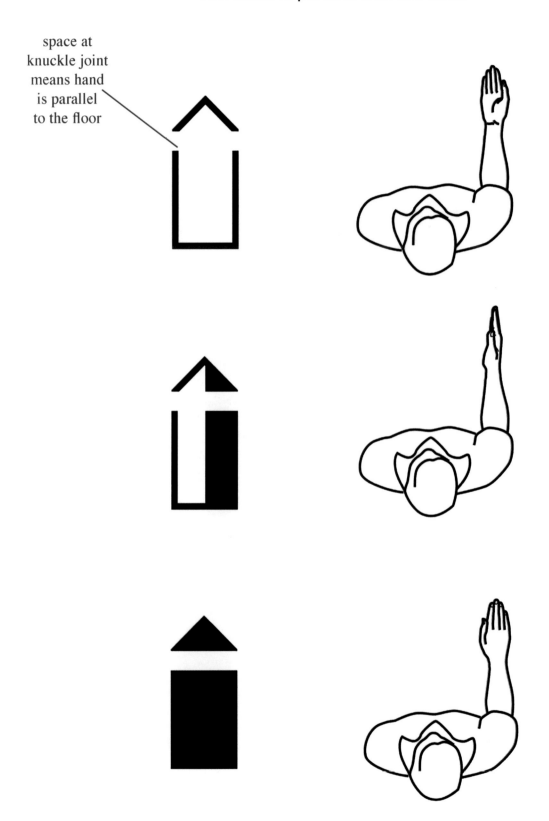

6 Contact Symbols

$*$ 1. Touch

$+$ 2. Grasp

|$*$| 3. Between

$\#$ 4. Strike

⊙   5. Brush

@   6. Rub

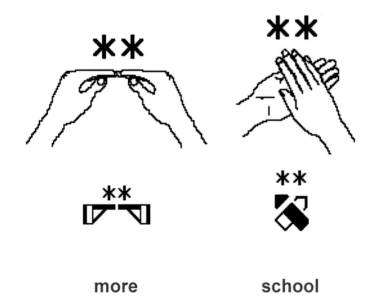

more   **school**

Touch

Touch Contact is written with an asterisk.

Touch is defined as the hand gently contacting another part of the body.

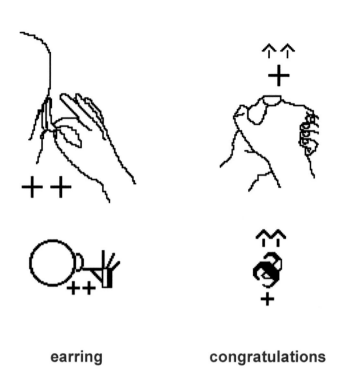

earring **congratulations**

✚
Grasp

Grasp Contact is written with two crossed lines.

Grasp is defined as the hand grasping or pinching a part of the body or a prop, such as clothing.

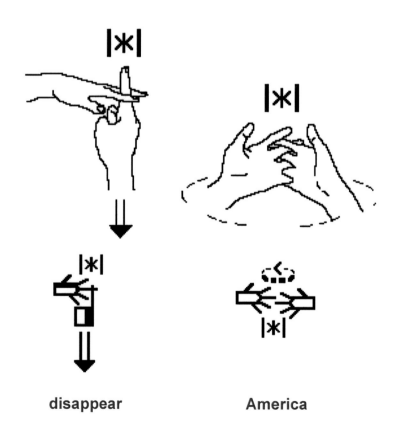

disappear **America**

|✱|
Between

Between Contact is written with a Contact Symbol between two lines.

Between is defined as contacting between two fingers or other parts of the body.

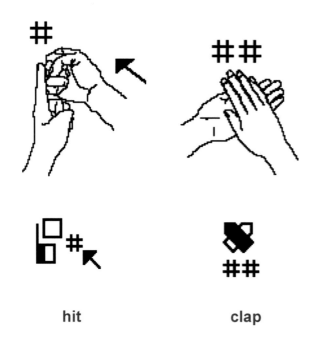

Strike

hit   **clap**

Strike Contact is written with two lines crossing two lines.

Strike is defined as the hand contacting a surface **with force**.

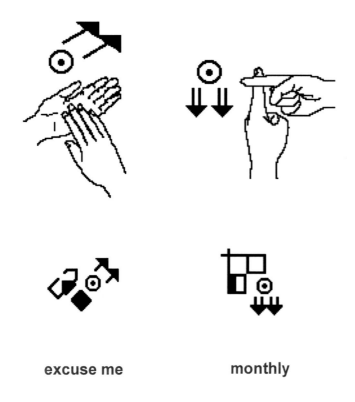

Brush

excuse me   **monthly**

Brush Contact is written with a circle with a dark dot in the center.

Brush is defined as movement that first contacts and then **moves off** the surface.

Circular
Rub

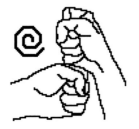

coffee

chocolate

Circular Rub Contact is written with a spiral.

Rub is defined as contact that moves, but **stays on the surface**.

Straight
Rub

neat

eager

Straight Rub Contact is written with the same spiral symbol, but the spiral symbol is **connected with a straight arrow**.

When the Rub Contact symbol is **connected with an arrow**, it rubs in a straight line (not in a circle). It stays on the surface but moves in the direction of the arrow.

6 Finger Symbols

⬢   1. Squeeze, Middle Joint Closes

⬡   2. Flick, Middle Joint Opens

˅   3. Hinge, Knuckle Joint Closes

˄   4. Hinge, Knuckle Joint Opens

˄˄˄   5. Hinge, Knuckles Open & Close Together

〰〰   6. Trill, Knuckles Open-Close Alternating

⬢ ⬡

Middle Joint
Squeeze & Flick

Middle Joint Finger Movements, also called Squeeze and Flick Movements, are written with small dots.

˅ ˄

Knuckle Joint
Hinge & Trill

Knuckle Joint Finger Movement, also called Hinge and Trill Movements, are written with small arrows.

Middle Joint
Closes

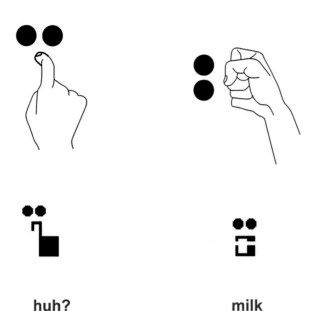

huh?

milk

When the middle joint of the finger squeezes tight (bends down or in), this **closing finger movement** is written with a **dark dot**.

The dot is placed near the finger joint that does the squeezing. Two dots represent two squeezes..

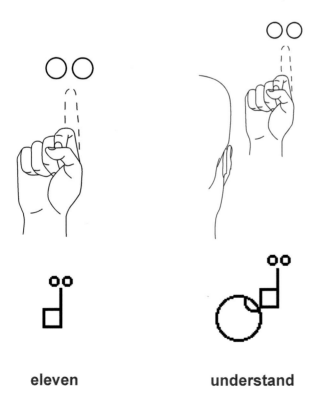

eleven

understand

Middle Joint
Opens

When the middle joint of the finger flicks open (goes from bent to straight), this **opening flicking movement** is written with a hollow dot.

The dot is placed near the finger that flicks. Two dots represent two flicks.

Knuckle Joint

Closes

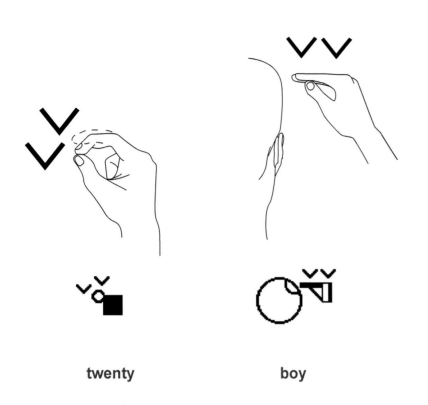

twenty   boy

The middle joint of the finger locks, while the knuckle joint bends down, like the Hinge on a door. This **closing knuckle movement** is written with a small arrow that points down. The arrow **pushes** the fingers down. Two arrows mean 2 hinges.

Knuckle Joint

Opens

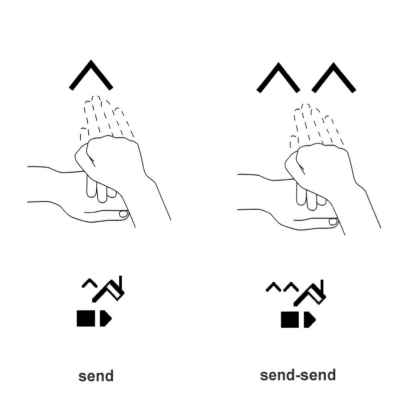

send   send-send

The middle joint of the finger locks, while the knuckle joint bends up, like the Hinge on a door. This **opening knuckle movement** is written with a small arrow that points up. The arrow **pulls** the fingers up. Two arrows mean 2 hinges up.

Knuckle Joints
Open-Close

The fingers move together in the same direction, as a unit. The knuckle-joints of the fingers open and close (bend up and down) together. This **open-close knuckle movement** is written with one row of small connected arrows pointing up and down.

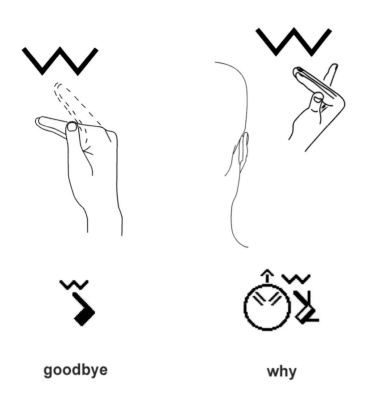

goodbye

why

Knuckle Joints
Alternate

The fingers do not move together in a unit. Instead they hinge in opposite directions. One moves up, as the other moves down. This **Alternating Finger Movement,** also called **Finger Trills**, is written with two rows of small arrows pointing up and down.

fingerspell

typing

Up-Down Movement

Up-Down Movement is parallel with the Front Wall or your chest.
It is written with double-stemmed arrows:

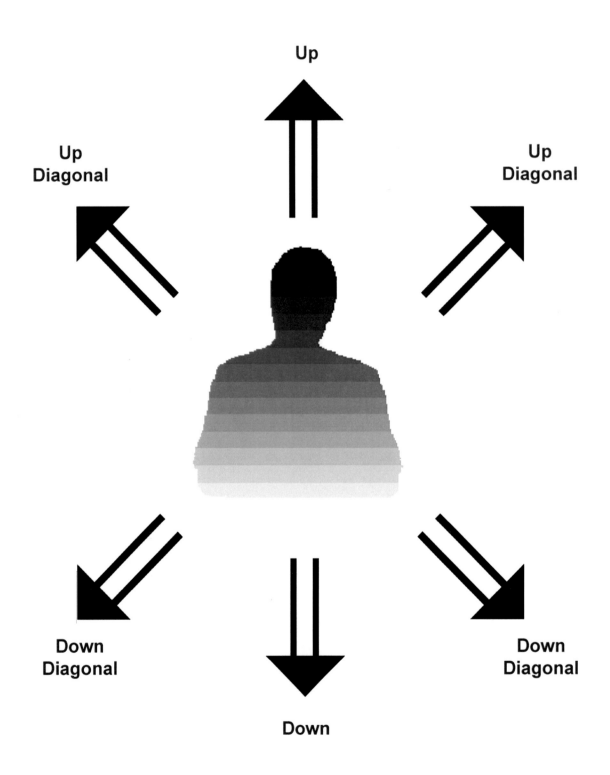

Forward-Back Movement

Forward-Back Movement is parallel with the Floor or a table top.
It is written with single-stemmed arrows:

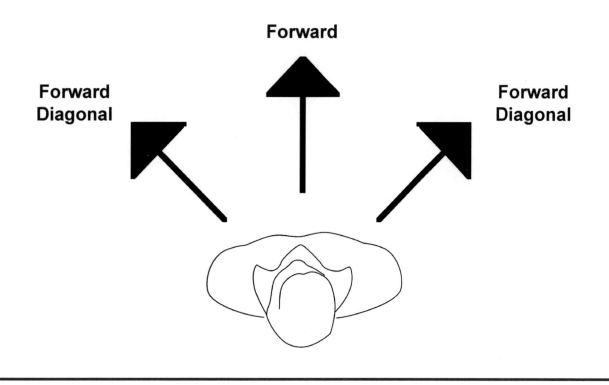

Forward

**Forward
Diagonal**

**Forward
Diagonal**

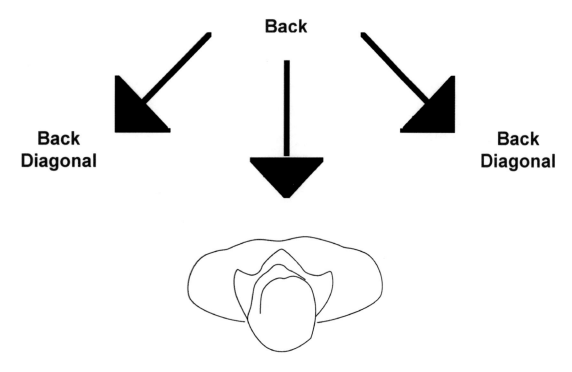

Back

**Back
Diagonal**

**Back
Diagonal**

Movement With The Right Hand
A dark arrowhead.

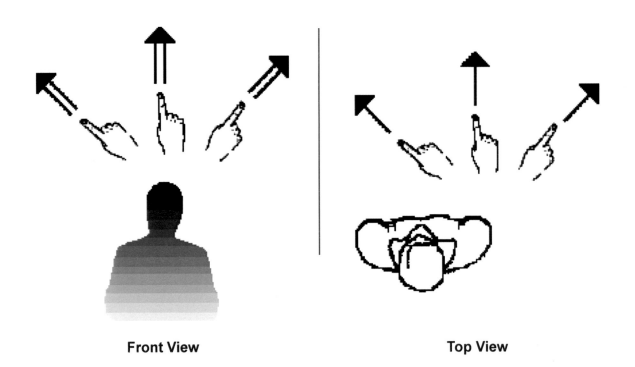

Front View   **Top View**

Movement With The Left Hand
A light arrowhead.

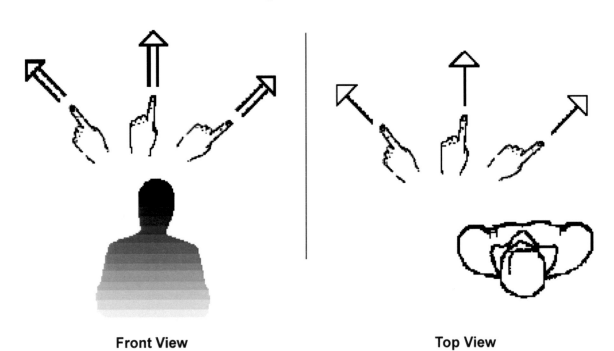

Front View   **Top View**

Movement To The Side

Movement to the side can be viewed from either the Front View or the Top View. It can be written with either double-stemmed or single-stemmed arrows.

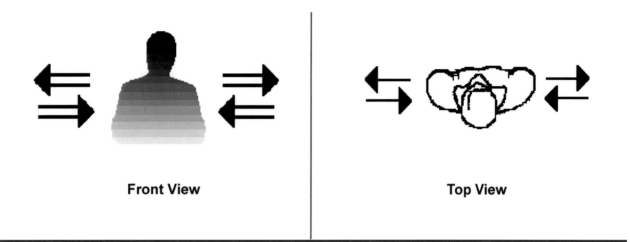

Front View   **Top View**

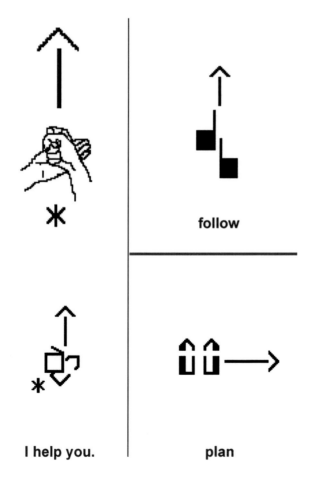

I help you.	plan

(follow)

General Arrowhead Writes Overlapping Paths

When a right movement arrow writes **ON TOP OF** a left movement arrow, the two movement paths **overlap each other**. The two arrows blend together. The dark arrowhead and the light arrowhead become one arrowhead, called the **General Arrowhead**.

Often the hands are contacting when moving in overlapping paths, but it is **NOT ONLY** for contacting hands. For example, two hands can be parallel, side by side, without contact, and then both move to the same side, so that the right arrow writes on top of the left arrow. This creates a **General Arrowhead**.

Do not confuse these arrows:

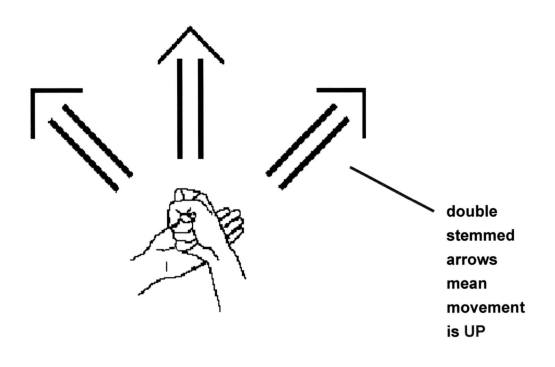

double
stemmed
arrows
mean
movement
is UP

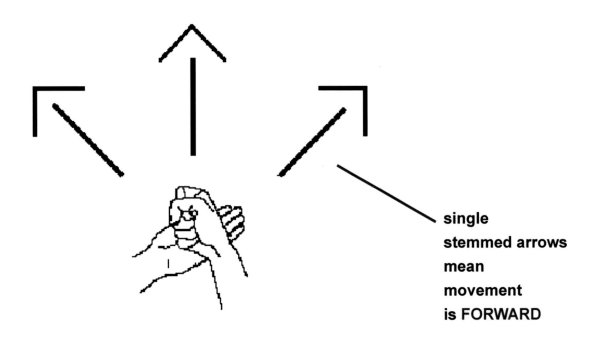

single
stemmed arrows
mean
movement
is FORWARD

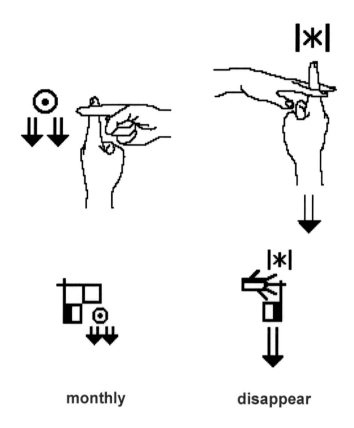

Straight Movement

Up or Down

A double-stemmed arrow means that the movement is straight up or down, parallel with the front wall. The movement is flat with the front of your body.

monthly   **disappear**

Straight Movement

Forward or Back

A single-stemmed arrow means that the movement is forward or back, parallel with the floor. You are looking down, on top of the movement.

excuse me   **eager**

Front View
Hands parallel with the Front Wall.

one half	Deaf	where

Top View
Hands parallel with the Floor.

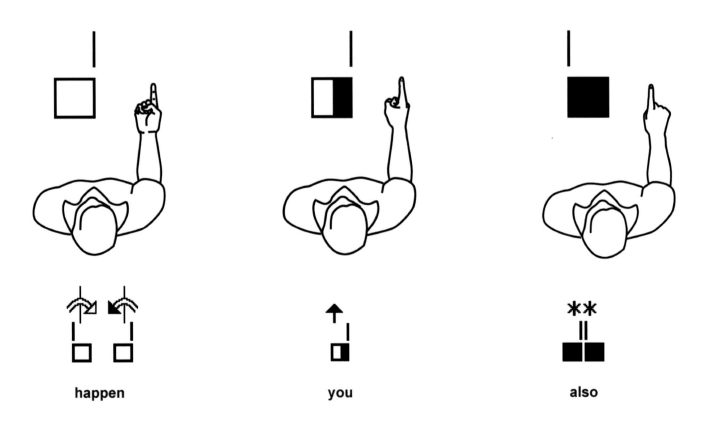

happen	you	also

Front View
Hands parallel with the Front Wall.

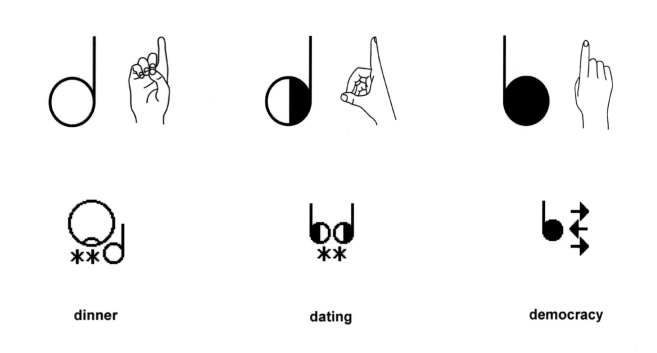

dinner   dating   democracy

Top View
Hands parallel with the Floor.

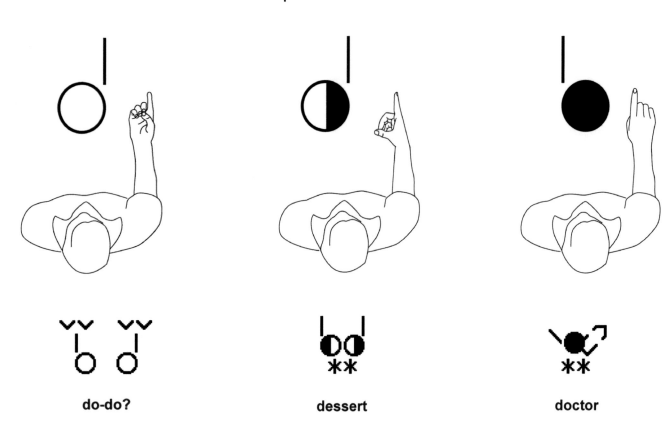

do-do?   dessert   doctor

Front View
Hands parallel with the Front Wall.

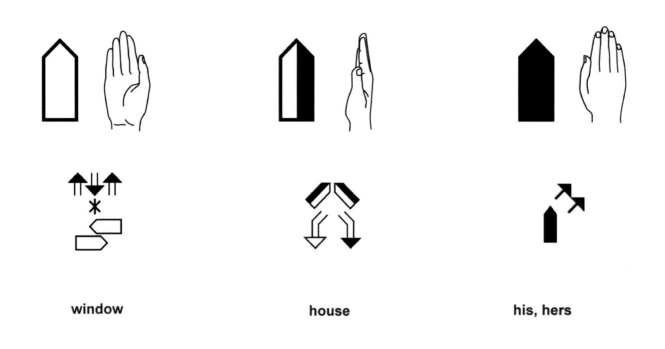

window   house   his, hers

Top View
Hands parallel with the Floor.

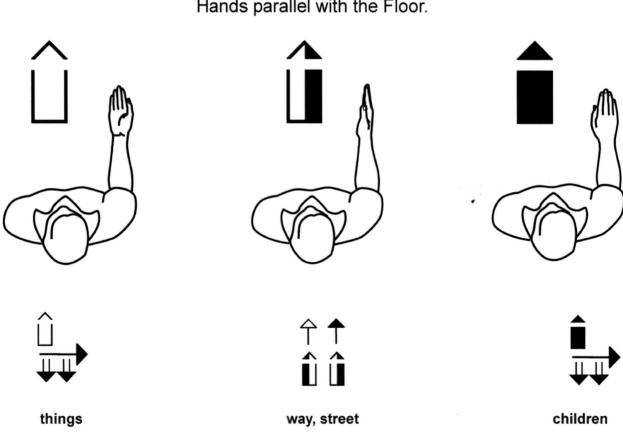

things   way, street   children

Pause,
Comma

Period,
End of
Sentence

English Translation: Writing ASL from the Deaf perspective.

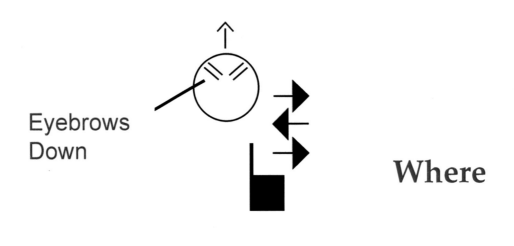

Eyebrows
Down

Where

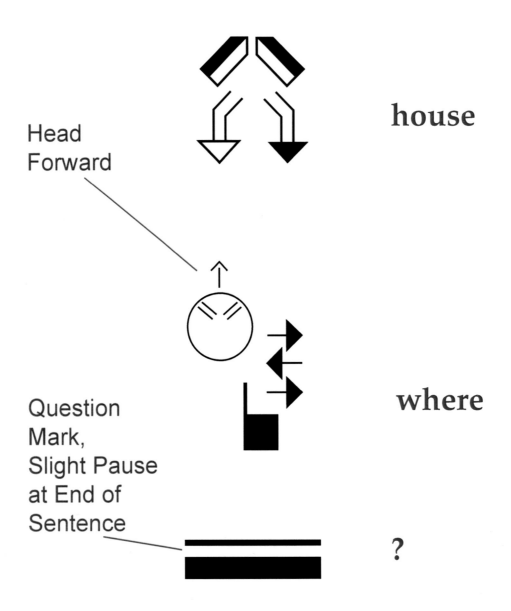

Head
Forward

house

Question
Mark,
Slight Pause
at End of
Sentence

where

?

English Translation: Where is the house?